IS AN ARSENAL ENOUGH TO·FREE AN ORCHARD? SWAMPTHING,

INEBRIATE. I'LL ARM A GARDEN. WE CAN ALL LIVE THERE.

AHSAHTA PRESS
BOISE, IDAHO
2014

THE NEW SERIES

#64

BEAST FEAST

CODY-ROSE CLEVIDENCE

Ahsahta Press, Boise State University, Boise, Idaho 83725-1525
ahsahtapress.org
Cover design by Quemadura / Book design by Janet Holmes
Printed in Canada

LIBRARY OF CONGRESS CATALOGING-IN-PUBLICATION DATA

Clevidence, Cody-Rose, 1984–
[Poems. Selections]
Beast feast / Cody-Rose Clevidence.
pages cm.—(The new series ; #64)
Summary: "BEAST FEAST offers opposition to the Emersonian mythology of peaceful Nature by suggesting
the histories of cruelty and commodity that inhabit the forests of America. By supposing the 'weirdness' of
nature—which includes the weirdness of humans and animals in their bodies—the poems in this collection
evoke the the sense of immediacy of being, accidentally, 'in the world' of history, capital, bodies, laws, desires,
and phenomena"—Provided by publisher.
ISBN-13: 978-1-934103-53-1 (pbk. : alk. paper)
ISBN-10: 1-934103-53-5 (pbk. : alk. paper)
1. Nature--Poetry. I. Title.
PS3603.L498.A6 2014
811'.6—dc23
2014020850

ACKNOWLEDGMENTS

I'd like to thank the editors of the journals where some of these poems first appeared: Megan Garr at *Versal*, Jennifer Nelson at *Epiphany*, C. Violet Eaton at *Bestoned*, Matt Henriksen at *Cannibal* & for everything he does, the folks at *Aufgabe* for being so consistently awesome. Also Thurston Moore at Flowers & Cream Press for releasing the little silver chapbook "everything that is beautiful is edible," which contained a lot of the poems that would become *BEAST FEAST*. & Thanks to Cole Swensen, Lee Ann Brown, Caroline Crumpacker & Rebecca Wolff for harboring me, either in workshops or in the world. & so much thanks to Janet Holmes and all the people at Ahsahta for making a space for this book among the other beautiful & interesting books they publish.

I'd like to especially thank my brilliant friends for being brilliant and also my friends: Jane Gregory, Sara Nicholson, Chris (C. Violet) Eaton, Kevin Holden, Elaine Khan, Thera Webb, Amelia Jackie (The Molasses Gospel), Mel Elberg, Elise Kaufman, Carson Hines, & Franny—my endless thanks for shaping my brain. & thanks to all the queer land projects that are & provide habitat, especially to Sacha at Fancyland for providing me with the space & time to work on this project.

& thanks to my dad, mother & stepdad, after forcing me on all those "nature" walks & arguing Plato with me over dinner. What else could you have expected.

ABOUT THE AUTHOR

Cody-Rose Clevidence graduated from the Iowa Writers Workshop & lives (mostly) in the Arkansas Ozarks with their dog, Pearl.

FOR FRANNY

*[words in use in the world are in conversation & are erecting certain structures of thought in relation to the world & to other uses of these words & this is an argument re: "natural" "animal" "world" etc.]

CONTENTS

[elegiac wtf glibness you lion you
full in the blueness caused by a chance encounter—
drunkard— pebble— dream on or dream me a reaper full
of wine or whatever— blood— vital full frontal
bullet-proof forest— I'm densing there— amassing there
Ozark & hammer— leapt from rhyme— I call
out— beam— through to the silent— there is an eagle
all alone.

the pure the fetid swamps dear the cool earth guilty lay down
in break or broken day, dream— blue shock dismal— triumph— river.

far from the brackish & impotent swagger & sludge of my home
I'll slander & hunch down deep call me a swill of a city I'll fuck her for dizzy
for blueness I'll drink it— etched gull in dark water— grim slip & silence to
   plod through
I'll take it— glee— shake of mane— a switch cut— a sharpened edge to live on.]

[THIS THE FOREST]

monoglottal polylimbic slightly amorous
loose-lipped, spurned a grunt from flower
precambrain multiplicity in the densing
postapocalyptic forest wolf me down.

multivalent deluge in the nether regions
bi-polar supersonic vast visceral nets cast
this defunct etymology of tongue-tied
neanderthalithic croon tender & prone.

all diachronic many-petaled yes gentle
slipshod continent spinning a drift gifted
anticipatory polymorphic glee a bizarre
wild synapse in numerous crowned skin,

listen orchestral architecture listen neural
network, wire, branch, spark, pent-up multip
licitious postures, covalent hued sky, diaphanous
masculinity, low polyphonic human drone

rhizomic, lightly soiled, multigendered lily of
hypersexual ungraceful fluxuation, amassing in
mutagenic saprophytic bud all gown, strut o
lunge into this the forest where all nature's dethroned.

E|Ros|ion— x. *is a stutter in the tail feathers* Optic (*verse*) is as *irridesce* in the pure force I am in love with an error / *gem.* is glory & *graphic* [] *sic.* is prefixed like as in EYEBALL [to claim] "the open"— {all ownership//theft} & {gory there} *is tarred* w. {history} in the derelict plumage "*what wet sky the sun is stolen from*" & I am a thief [&will be criminal] [diurnal] [in excess] {*of x*} the pure force *versus* the embodied force {the force of bodily being} *we must remove ourselves from the meadow unless*— this is the squalid & the pigeon infested, leaden, pcb-laden, irradiated, is the only—{I am so healthy I could shit a dove} *all placement is displacement* [to claim] [no State] [especially not a natural one] my peacock voluptuous w. ~~femininity~~ ~~masculinity~~ [virile is as volatile does] *leuc.* "to strut into the open" *to be denied is the only*— is a mutant {body}/ x. in the junked [recesses] *accretion* {THE ACCUMULATED FORCE}   how pristine—

o)))))))))))))

to see & not be implicated in the seeing
to see & not to give the seeing back to yourself in words   [is/is not
human]

::YELLOW FLOWER: BITTER PETAL:: ::THAT THERE IS NO SACRED THING::

to see an object is to distinguish
to see an object is to extinguish

to dampen optic
hide ontic seed

.

to know & then to see *versus* to see & then to know;
to know w/o seeing, & vice versa, etc.

in the foveal landscape appear small & fractured roots.
in the vulgar landscape appear many small & fractured roots.

in the land there is many flecks of eyes.
in the land there are many flecks of eyes.

a fetished gaze sets forth all prism in the deed.
to see an object is to relinquish.

the deeds to the eyes of the land are x-ed out
the deeds to the land are liars indeed

the dead, deeded land a seen unseeded need,
secedes the eyes. in piles, blinks.

in the land there is many flecks of eyes.

        how long does it take the head of a bird to rot when it is in a
sealed container   versus   how long it takes to rot when it is left in
the meadow. when it is buried in the meadow? when it is suspended in
the sky?

        how long does it take the head of a bird to rot when
it is submerged in the ocean, in a cold river, in a bucket. when it's
nailed to a tree. in the desert. when it's on fire, when it is still alive?

.

to cultivate a sense of the many senses needed to sense the many
things—
                    versus to cultivate a way to parse the world into
sensible objects

        [is/is not human]

the ability to see & the graceful inability not to see, [indicative of pre-
existing structures of sight]

having a ripe : a draped form indicates
  to lay across the surface of the seen

each earth comprises : is huge : is
  unripe or undefined edge

.

[to beat oneself repeatedly against the hard surface of the earth
which is ±132,000 ft thick   ] to suffer bruises . . .

ACRID ROOT BLEEDS SHINE BLEEDS PINK   RUB IT ON YOUR
XXX

a corroded   animalia : ooo mourn morn oiled trench oiled eye
tissue = vault | blue = blue | harm = forest   more thrust than need
less trust than treason

[less lust than reason] or [less reason than lust]
or, [roughly ≈]

I have a triple helix in the form of a prison
  many dead birds in my cellular structure

many dead deeds lay lying: lay singing
  a lying dead debtor song.

many small prisons in the interstitial tissues
  fails : gems : horizonal   is no asylum—

lasso   cuss is an animal to be skinned here   verily
micro-vulnerability   I am calling but the animals never come
& offer themselves to my knife . . .

.

to speak with the belief that words = things
to speak [is/ is not] to eat the objects around you

to speak = a dime
to speak = an apple

to speak = a sort of moaning
to speak = to utilize abstract & symbolic sounds to refer to things,
concepts & feeling in relation to the world around you.

to speak = a sort of complicated moaning
a groan is a grown man, gowned

to speak in one hand & shit in the other
     "& see which fills up first"
       [Themis]

.

    I have an oil rig in my persimmon. you are no secret palace nor
chariot to the scabrous castle. you are no sky, neither sky nor prince nor
weapon. I have a diamond but I hate it. I want to lick the machines of
war   "to be visible... is to be concrete & specific" "objects lack color
in the dark" . what triumphant battalion drowns itself in the crowned
(crowded) seas. androgyne. confusion. many people have a necessary
violence.

"the gaze of power" "the politics of vision" "an object of vision: a sight" "mirror gaze" decide= to cut. "I see the world objectively" *I see the colors unbounded from their forms* . . . (bullsh*t)—hypothetical & intrinsic re-evaluation suffers as needed.

I have a skinned eye
I have a skinned "I"

I have an I made out of skin
I have an eye which is a hole in my skin.

I have an I made out of many eyes, compiled.
each blink joins the blinking. each blink is a seed,
"un petite mort"—a recalibration.

I have (an) ox-eye daisy(ies) scattered over the surface of the world.

there is no making sense of the senseless
except with what senses you sense with

skin my eye touch tongue my greed is
historic, odorous & loud.

[the gaze that holds us in reveals
us to us reviles us]

[you must teach yourself to like the everything that is allowed]

.

when there is a singular experience its ripples form ambiguities around
it.

when there is an ambiguous experience its singularity forms ripples
around it.

each sound joins the multitudes of endlessly rippling sound
surrounding us.

it is a deafening city.

these apples are full of madness.

.

peel pears for eyes, ears, heal
pealed belted rung out : to void

is to laid down; to laid bare : sight
   bare in the vital organs: mouths

  to peel the heaven from the wordless
   fruit : buried . it peeled me there

  to succumb in the deed of succumbing is to
  lay flat on the transversed surface
     you transverse.

my apples are full of madness.
each daisy is looking out at us.

each daisy has the perennial eye of a [the] [nonexistent] god.

IXIST?

u red u read my eat this neck wrung dear Archimedes—what killed
sprout an egregious IAMB, damn—u verbed it GOOD. u et it.

no really u cn have 1(one) free proposition b4 anomaly   it had better be
logically sound. not like echo not like traverse & not like phenomena.

u cn choke on yr play-doh u read.

.

XIETY—

zircon & bassoon over cocooning river, glossiolier, gasoline &
pilfer, dumbass, swoon.

.

X (LUT)
Origin:
< L, neut. pl. treated as if fem. sing.

$$$$$$ now we are free dear drear rock-doves (schist shit-pigeons city-
bound cuckolded ringéd-eyed semiquavers) (a little hustle) "baby I got
yr money" /// a free crease in the bodily economy. what free, trash-
birds, is reliance? a lily-white stain on the night's bounty yr insipid
moral harbor & ring.

ILXID

Ov u have robbed it us, of the binding thing, u who loved . we [who hate &] fall back from loves as grains from stalks into our own chaste nothingness.

.

IEVE
Origin:
< Sp, dim. of gola throat

I is all like livid, the residue of it, I is all like "ache" sour the sweet, bitter the brine, mine, & "oceanic". I is all like curr & cuss & press. now the adze of plenty the stroke of luck the marrow sucked & spit the man masked the uninhabitable made (almost) habitable. the fat the butter of the sky.

.

IXNAY

sar (tre) ble! (((o))) is motion, latin-ate, free is oh so & hollow, u fill, ufill w. red INK plz scarf until full a (w)hole what is a disgrace ingested—
        what retch(éd) carved-out & maketh "pure"

.

LIV/VIL

&c. the built in solid is a given—u warm little CREAture// is a claim,
what to make is stake a claim there— (no) what to touch is claim— (no)
{a new relation to ownership— } is a bodily—

        I mean it boldly will u give it to me>>>>>>>

.

VULT
<Informal . to play or trifle idly; fool

ure/ inure.

.

X(ULT)

u cn really rationalize this plethora? "literal" symbols? neural pain in
response to a blueness? I glut & my 'self' is all eroded into
            overgrowth. this metonymic thrust is all that thrusting is.

I'll break yr universal grammar w/ my anamorphic lust.

.

F (x)

an urgency or immediacy of being, slur, what crimson. dust the rubble
of a mouth. a bruise defines the boundary.

                              :: u con u verge in bee in ethereal pound ing
gloriole (())   v. noumen wrack/& phenom all a flutter,

                                        . . .

            a whole flock of 'em—

glit ver. *(f)* lisped river [heal't] wide crop to vulture   "cashmere"   battled-
over & unzipped carcass-relation earthward hulk.   in sno-blue be a pretty
boy, spin.   this ugly harp erodes the acred realm I built a palace in. f. only.
[aspen & quake]   yr "dire" need   eat dirt

lict. *v.* [ectonomy]   salivate along the edges of—   *noisia* hex-agonal plasmic-
microcosmic-embrace   be my divine aw shucks   divinity is a farce
careless inedible rock & taxonomy   sun-bathed lamé all crust all un-ontic
plumage xxx   derivative & delirious, "lush" like as in "drunk"   pre-mordant
vrr. [loop] & [loop]

be caustic deficient larva *def.* (nou) be holten   dew u are & dew u will be
&crud & tox. & algebraic, viral, "bowled over," poured out . [succumb'd to
necessity.] pack the mud around your eyes, silly, don't be craven, be brave [en]
(?). [z] throttle the throttle hum & then cry out

chock full of lustering vilt. [pre] fab. "luminosity" follow me into the "earth" (I
hate it there.) choke "up" *(mem.)* personified skyward unbuttoned cul-de-sac
sweet-pulp to eat   to gravel it ; roughen skin with. cusp all shock all blown
apart & fluted [lit.] "flow" *(rim)* from "ver" *across which*   [-zon] marsh is mire,
inmirrored, stalked— .

[HAMMER/TULIP]

hammer, tulip, aspirate you slut you wretch you lovely.
you voiceless glottal fricative, you beauty.

flesh this wild thing out. is syntactically
atrocious— I multiply to eyes a system in which

a panorama or else. diagram me a convulsive body
you field of trampled, you derelict amoral as a meadow.

gimme many petals. dire oxen pull to thrust out.
satin faggot is love so monotone anyone can hum it?

can anyone traipse as much as us?

++++

is an arsenal enough to free an orchard? swampthing,
inebriate. I'll arm a garden. we can all live there.

++++

there have always been a glitch like this
you absolute & urgent aria you angel you slag.

polychromatic multiplication along the ozone folds.
polyhedra in the interstice. diamond. rough cut

carved from a formal neoclassical marble. you tease you tempest
you pansy-blooded plethora on whose stalk grows polymorphic fruit,

anathema to "form".

++++

        listen, dimwit. I'm an animal
        with pretty much no short term memory
        & a penchant for shiny things.

++++

idyll my dandy, petunia, massacre. carniferous
polyglottal pulch. what harm is done to a body.

lewd slew & throng is a messy *genitalia* be my *reductio ad infinitum*
hussy of formless furrow the acreage you ugly unseeded desire spit to the wind &

what ~~palace~~ — forest— Tend.

[. . . .]

  antennae zoned circumference homoerotic perfume
giddy hazard pony. slack dialect of breeze lut giddyup all brack
ish or pulver. eye all wild zone. all lip to clawed
                    negation of country.

  necessitates a radicalized language. inside the inner ligament
of zero huh glitter all sequin percussion the landscape. bark scrape a wet
knee of being. flute maim an optic toward vision. all tulip limb
               is succumb, combat, whim.

  pomegranate is many many many & seed shine forth filthy
skin cut from slime all electric fuck a cathedral. snag meta
entranced slur spawn microclimate all glory. culled happenstance
             from a wrought endeavor—

  all filly bred from mammalian haute couture. Aphrodite,
iris a full blown pithic volt is perversity citified. be a god
damn ingot before a broken mannequin of field, stumble.
            is many (&c) sensic note.

I planted 19 karats • I am a golden gravel-eater • there is a fleur in my styx •
the teeth of history still exist in the ground & in the systems we live [within] •
I would like to utter some words now • but I can't utter any utterance w/o first
uttering an excuse • I am vegetative in my innermost colors • I have an entire
handful of dirt probably with some shit in it & the work of many generations
of worms • there is some myx in my nectar • this lush inheritance • forest
growed on "such strange fruit" • on such mass migrations • how can we even
• at all • how can I • the clearing is thick w. pre-existing forest • I am un-
open in the clearing in which one is supposed to be open • un-open in the very
clearing-which-is-supposed-to-be-metaphorical-for-the-being-of-being-open-in-
the-clearing • I unopen myself with such a hardness it is pretty metal • in my
deepest darkest innards there is a tarnished & fearful rat • somewhere there is a
lizard in there • in what capacity do I claim an ability to do things like love • I
have no crystalline structure that I know of • not a stitch of divinity to justify
this • I promise to never call this [my] gravel worthy • I promise to only plant
these [my] shitty seeds in this [my] lead-heavy soil • to never call these seeds
geometric • prismatic • mathematical • "beautiful" • to never count them •
to never name their colors • I promise to eat the heavy metals from the fruits &
leaves that grow in this [my] [only] dirt • because this is the world •

BEAST BEATS SELF AGAINST CRUSTAL EARTH

*

BEAST EATS MONEY, SHITS GOLD.

*

BEAST EATS SMALLER (OR LARGER), DUMBER BEASTS.

*

BEAST GETS A NECKLACE & IS BEAST, ADORNED.

*

BEAST PAWS SATIN, CHEWS MUD. BEAST SHEDS, SWEATS, SPITS, FUCKS,
SWOONS.

*

BEAST HAS URGES. OXYTOCIN, NOREPINEPHRINE, DOPAMINE,
ADRENALINE. BEAST MODULATES IN RELATION TO XIR ENVIRONMENT.
BEAST REELS IN POSTSYNAPTIC HAZE.

*

BEAST IS AN ELECTRICAL BEAST, FEELS LIKE A FLESHY BEAST (OR VICE
VERSA.)

*

BEAST IS DRIVEN TO IRRATIONAL INSTINCTS BY SMELLS & PHYSICAL
SENSATIONS. BEAST IS A HYPOTHESIS OF ANTICIPATORY BEHAVIORS.
BEAST ROLLS IN THE GOLDENROD & THEN IN THE BLUEBELLS & THEN IN
THE ROTTEN CARCASS OF ANOTHER BEAST.

*

BEAST IS A FILTHY, AMORAL ABSTRACTION WITH NO DIGNITY. BEAST
GORGES BEASTLINESS ON THE FATTY FRUITS OF THE LAND.

.

Beast of prefix gnaws on the garden of beasts. beast is grafting
beastliness into rootstock ripe for ripening. beast for occlusion.
beast for temporality. urgent beast in the urgency of beasting.
ungentle & urgent beast.

.*"the inclusion and capture of a space"*

The growl in the middle of words is the growl in the middle of
a meadow & by this the meadow is the zero of the growl in the
middle is the clearing of, &, poppies—

Beast of kindness beast of beasting. in the burdensome history
of beasting where there was a historical beast before there was
a human in the beasting forest. in the forest where the forms of
beasts are, &, made— be it a made thing in the beast of things.

."abandons the living being to law"

The zone exists as an enclosure, as an *'exclosure'*; 'scape &
by this the xeric is a liaison where every speaking implicits
a necessity— an emptying of 'the snarl' *as* necessity— is
releasing it into the lily's trumpet-like throat.

Non mons glottal non pubis to be less than a beast-meadow-
full is to draw a zero around this & the zero is mouthing. this
is where "to clear" (grunt-like) *"to clearing"* is profusion in the
sudden beast. "beast." the inarticulation before the articulation
as gesture, scent. is the happenstance of fur—

."the concussion and rapture of a space"

Beast of unnecessary forms beast of soliloquies beast for
slaughter beast in the city of scarcity beast of neuronal cordage
beast of burden. beast of preexisting beasts beast for glamour.
beast of knowing the being of beasting & beast of knowing the
beastliness of beasting & beast of not knowing. uproot the

garden of description into the anomic garden. where there were
beasts now there are beasts.

The edge of the zero in which necessity is a living mouth—
which exists, *so to speak*— as scraping out the inside of the zone
by a raw impulse is to establish the vicinity of the mouth which
is the zero the fluctuating rim of which is the clearing out of the
clearing

.*"beyond which shelter and safety are not possible"*

Beast for loneliness beast of distance. coppiced beast is a garden
in the forest. beast of occasional grimace beast of multiplicity
beast claims a exigent thrust in all directions. unlawful beast is
the utterance by which a necessary flower groans.

Here is the crude lip of the border & the crude lip of the beast
that gnaws on the border. the inevitable disappearance of the
forest. the extinction of beasts & the extinction of humans &
the urgency of evading the law as the only zone in which— is
the only animal—

& also the necessity of crudeness, & the necessity of beasts, & of degradation—lulled in the lullaby of the multifarious garden of beasts— all open eyes are the eyes of the forest in which a happening brings forth—

.

."*the threshold of indifference between anomie and law*"

The lip which is the rim which is the edge which is the eye which is the hesitation of the meadow & the hesitation of its unknown capacity for the forms of beasts, breathes.

Nominally, all the zones are interstitial in moonlight, bright beasts of illicit need. haughty & illiterate beasts of mutant beastliness— to suck the marrow of the cracked bones [to be sovereign] —to "live"

."*aimed at capturing pure being in the meshes of the logos*"

You beast in the logical marshes ensnared— the beautiful &/
or brutal carnivorisnesses— clawing at the need— which is a
home for many small beasts. the zero is a gnawed out interior in
which wind—in which what little abstraction—each beast must
gnaw their own zero—nevertheless—there is an indefinite howl
emitted by all the open mouths of flowers—in which live the
necessary beasts— in which lives the necessity of beasting—

Insufficient beast posits some more beasts. beast is tending the
amorphic garden. there are too many clearings in the forest.
there are too many beasts in the forest. there are too many
forests in the beasts. each beast must lay down in the meadow.

. "all the animals are gone"

STEER

AS ~~STAG~~ BECOMES

{   XEMPT // TRI-FORESTED // LANCED   }
is silicon that grows these budding trees
my heart-mascaraéd "heavens"

AS ~~STAG~~BULLOCK {TULIP} : CUNT IN THE ~~PERSPEC~~
          VIE | -dysmorphic | OF THE FETAL BULL
{ungenome-me (in) the striking(forth)}

                    ::

so horns velvet
my perseid form, up from the ground—
        {get}
//
peach-fuzz the budding horns
my tongue-tied nausea of form
"forest" ~~my royal,~~ hunting
~~ground~~

     ::

~~KING~~

SIRLOIN

STERIODAL // HYMNAL // {LASHES} DRENCHED IN THE
~~CELESTIAL~~ PLUMAGE : skirt
steak : fatback : eyelids blued w. sky
w. "feeling"

—in which I have implanted several
gems under the subcutaneous bark—

              hunter
      { smut & ~~gather~~ // anther under u
saprophytic // ~~rib~~ }
              eye'd trophic- bait
      & "switch"

u sapling u—

              ::

suet rubbed on skin. lard 2 polish the sky w. 2 lure the does w.

::

I SHED MY NEW ANTLER

YELLOW IN THE SUNLIGHT

BULLIED AS A DIAMOND IS SOW SOWN U HOARSE

PERVERSE W. CROCUS

::

what [] permeates the matter
xacerbates the 'zure gonads
are heisted // bedazzled—

hyperreal w. synthetic pearls

o my doe sweet as grass-
fed beef o my lily-white
ass & lucre shined eye-
bright my golden god damn-
nation o my love

salt in the nostrils &
mud in yr stud Orion.

[DAWN WAS CROWNING FUCK THE KING
HIS CORPOR{REAL
            RATE} FORM & FACELESS MATH
& ZENITH JARGON HAPPENSTANCE. MY RIGID [COCK]
DISSOLVES INTO A FIELD OF BLUETS & FURTHER TO ANAPHORA, REEK
OF PISS ON GRASS. THIS MEADOW IS MY ONLY FACE. I GRAZE UPON IT.]

u blue-balled aeon shocked in heat my virile dalliance-encrusted earth
I swoon the gas-slick'd & billous smoked, the tiny lights of cities a distant
necklace strung. I am asleep in the forest of lights while endless numbers
flick & crash & surge. the trees drop nuts the ferns spore the bees have sex
with flowers. this diversified monotony I puke & press against
my mossy pillow, my toxic diet, my creatural body's heat.
u oil'd river u yolk & ooze u soiled masculinity "divine". u fatty fat
fat beauty. u daisy-studded nasdaq. u "being in the world".

BEDECK'D W. JOULES O IN OCHEROUS LIGHT STORM-RIDDEN & "SWEPT"
THOUGH GULLET $$$'S PERVERSE: IS MY OZONE ENOUGH TO HOLD US—

THIS FORLORN, THIS LOINÉD FLUENCE, CUT A BLEEDY SEEDLING SAP
ALL RED AGAINST THE BLACKISH LOAM MY DEARLING UP & GO.

IS NEED A NEST TO BED A SWALLOW IN?

ENDLESS HOLOZOIC CRAWLT THE CALCITE SURFACE, NIBBLING
& SPOON ME "ZZZ," A NETTLE BED, A POSTAPOCALYPTIC PASTURE, O.

WHAT MONOSYLLABIC UTTERANCE A
PROKARYOTA IS ALL SLIME NO NUT ALL URGE— &
EVEN ULTRAVIOLET FEATHERS, EVEN STRUMPET-
COLORED LILIES, ASS-RED @ DAWN BABOONS, THE
PULSE OF HYPHAE THRU SOIL, COILING & UNCOILING
TONGUES OF POLLINATING INSECTS, LOW LONG
TONES RESONATING IN DEEP WATER, WHAT PREENED
SEED-PODS EXPLOSIVE RELEASE WHAT PHEREMONAL
SWEAT OF VINES & VIVID ROSES, VISCID SURFACES
ATTRACTING FLIES, BEES WHO "DANCE" RAMPANT
MIMICRY, RHYTHMIC LIT SIGNALS THROBBING IN
DARK CAVES, FLASHES IN DEEP WATER, EYELASHES,
WARNING TEETH & BLOODY GUMS & MOTHS THAT
LOOK LIKE FACES, LUNGE & BRISTLE, SHRIEK &
SCATTER "SNAKE" & "LEOPARD" LIMP-WRIST &
STRUTTED, SIGHED, THE HUMILIATED GRINNING,
FLUSH, BARED TEETH & COVERED EYES, LICK'D &
WHISTLED, ALL OF THIS & MORE & WHAT OF THESE
SIGNS SOUNDS OR GESTURES BIRTHS A SINGULAR
MATHEMATICS A LANGUAGE PRONE TO ....???
...............???...................... A LANGUAGE
THAT GIVES RISE TO LAW, ETC.

ooooooOOOoOOooOOOooOOOOOOOOOooooooOOOOOO
OOOOooOoOOOOOooooooooooOOOOooooooOOOOO
OOOOOOOOOOOOOOOOO)))))))))))) fruition// hush
Hesperides [oOooO] animosity {mossiness} {of the
anima} o be vowel// growl grown.

                                        <>

                                    grotesque &
mirrored noise mirroring noise   //   anamalistic vowel be
avowed & returning to the din   what language
"makes us human"   in the dilapidation of melody
in the net of noise encircling the earth—

"this one".

        <>

38

A STATE OF NATURE
A NATURAL STATE

\ ooo *"helianthus"* & *vulgaric*
~~sprung~~ Whatever grass. Here before you

Lain a *global meadow :*

    <<each flower represents a different global market & you, standing
in the meadow, can watch as the fluctuating market economy bows & twirls
& spouts & blooms. each stalk of grass or stem of flower a stock or share in a
mulinational graph of gubernational investments. each piece of trash represents
a city scattered among the daisies, burdock & violets. each bit of dirt, glass or
gravel represents a 'man'.

this symbolic horseshit is symbolic.
          this field is full of shit.>>

I want to own a gully, plant it full of guns.

\ "[acts committed during a state of exception] will be absolutely undecidable,
and the definition of their nature— whether executive or transgressive...
whether human, bestial, or divine— will lie beyond the sphere of law."

/wind driven & cruciferous
~~rational~~ animal.   volatile
~~animal~~.   homo sapien sapien
~~"DIVINE"~~

: NECTAR KILLER : MUSTARD SEED   : MACED OR MACERATED FACE :
U ILLEGAL STRUCTURE : FACE-PLANT U SUPINE COUNTRY :   U DOMIN-
ATRIXED FIELD : THISTLE : ALLERGIC   :   STUMBLT OVER BROKEN
METAL : U RASH :   DRUNK ON NOXIOUS WEEDS : BUILT A BOWER THERE

\now I will tell you how the dumb birds are supposed to fly.

\now I will tell you how the dumb big bucks are hunted.

\now I will tell you about the extreme stupidity of trees.

/now I will tell you how the brilliant markets glisten. The European & Asian
markets closed down some # points today, creating mountainous vertiginous
graphs all peaks & gullies surging.   The global economy is intricate & full of
signification, its glowing strands enlace the globe like veins, like skin, like the
electromagnetic field sparkling in the magellenic winds. Whole communities
live & die inside its rampant shifting ecosystem, strung along like pearls.

40

<<O value, weigh me, wrap me in yr dazzling pulsing blanket of numbers like a thousand blinking stars. I will transverse yr peaks & gullies, bathe in yr streams, drink from yr springs & eat the hyper-ripened fruit of yr symbolic trees.>>

\now I will tell you about the structures I've erected on the surface of the dumb earth to live inside of.

      || :: i radii poured cement & wept (j/k) – is a lol in the sovereign face— is a membrane of the Real— is kind of like whatever— hauled galvanized aluminum screwed nailed & stroked load-bearing beams thru which I erect a wound cut into the meadow— is my sovereign resistance embedded in dumb hard wood is my resistance a material stance:: ||

\"the power of the law lies precisely in the impossibility of entering into what is already open."

/ooo u *"nasty"* & *"dieseled"*
humongous chariot. Filth me to
define a Lily— is having a Tantrum
There.

\that the long white arm of the law is benumbed w. gems & strokes some lilies
gently—

\if you walk easily on its open palm, if you are permitted to the meadow of its
elbow, if you do not stumble under the weight of its forearm, then you—   . . .

/that revulsion is the violence that enforces.

        <<each flower in the meadow represents a different range of commodity
values & exchange rates expressed in supermarkets, grocery stores, outlet
centers, corner markets & vendor stalls across the globalized earth in-real time.
the gross market value of roses hovers between .0x¢ & .0y$ per doz. it fluctuates
in response to the markets of human emotions. if you stand in one spot long
enough you can watch as the flowers change value>>

<< I want to give my love a rose I want to love a growing thing w. petals I want to
love a stolen thing: a gross thing: an undefinable # >>

: LOAM EATER : LEAKT OPTICS FROM A SPIGOT : OXALIC : UNZONED
UNARCHETYPE UNLEGALY TENDER : &YET TENDER :   UNPASTURIZED
:   UR RAMPANT ANARCHISM :   LACED OR LACERATED FACE :   SLUT
OF THE MEADOW : U TRASH U UNBROKEN : THICKET :   THICKLY HELD

/biomimicry
~~exuberant~~ ~~harmonia~~
~~a state of nature~~
~~a natural State~~

\ "For the animal is in relation to his circle of food, prey, and other animals of its own kind, and it is so in a way essentially different from the way the stone is related to the earth upon which it lies. In the circle of the living things characterized as plant or animal we find the peculiar stirring of a motility by which the living being is "stimulated," *i.e.*, excited to an emerging into a circle of excitability on the basis of which it includes other things in the circle of its stirring."

/ in the depths of the forest you can hear the low moans & grunts & quickened panting of numbers propagating in the dark.

VERB/ATIM PURL <PURDY> PEALT FELL SAID FALL'D
FALLEN SULLEN MUZZLE. #PAN/OPOLECTIC OPAL'D
CUNT. X-PHRASIS VOID BE NUZZLED <HOPE>

TRANS/IS LUCENT "EYEBALL'D" HAIRY NIGHT <FELT>
'D FULVOUS QUEEN. @DAGGERED LILAC & @ A GLANCE
DENDRITIC UNDER "(THE) FULL MOONED LIGHT."

"I AM RINGING IN MY CHLOROPLASTS"— PRINCE
PRINCESS POLIS BACCAT SHOUT. DIG <DUG> GRIN
{HUMBLE'D} CERE/BELLIC FUSE & ION SPENT.

PURR "PURE" IN ORPHIC THORN'D SKIN SAID DIG
ROSE ROSE WHIP/ORWILL IN GUTSY BODIES FIX'D
IN M/EAGER <SOFT> & <SOIL> BUILT.

OZ | ARC *(noumen)* clutch. re: what I have said abt. Cavorting; w. frills. *NIL.*
[xchanged the moon 4 pears xchanged the pearls 4 milk xchanged the mono- for
polysaccardides xchanged the stars 4 imaginary genitalia & syntax 4 grafted
cultivars]

ZERO | SUM *(mal.) lickt.* vis. "grease" & "sap" & "melody"

[alleged junk]- *vie.x* (&tyx) –a corruption in the mountainous (desire) re: *Sulc.*
plethora'd creeping streams "r" all "asunder" w. pronominal excess, shaken
out like drops in light. *fusc.* UN | POLISHT it 2 rough 2 play. [xer] & [zilch]
&[forested] - 2 tough 2 chew

E | R | Oar : *mulch'd; "to fermented":* this wine-as-sweet-as-skin-is-salty   as
bodied-is-as-bodied-do *ilc.* Re: what I have made w. tools :   gold-finch'd
enclosure :   bows lashed to beams : I see yr tooth marks in the soil [*xyd>*
re: "how to build" ; something about continuance] [is constant erosion]

N. | *lvd* set a radiant *pelt. re: v. ile'd* "lust" re: IN | VOLUT nail'd & leveled into
geometry   & set it there "to gather" *(s.pit: is lucid in:verse(D)re:elation)* n. Xis
–ist. [xchanged the sinew 4 signs & signifiers & back again]

 THINGS I WILL PLACE :   glass in some relation to the sun | warmth in
some relation to the night.

this is antagonistic this is microscopic this is a clamoring range a
high-yield perverse impulse lower, lower, lower, flower—

this is a baited this is a yearning in the soil this is latent violence
in limb, tooth, grin—this is clawful I told him I am not ignorant
of the claw.

is this a gated garden is this ambivalent is this a penultimate river
this is a mutant form of something I've seen before, leave it

or take it. is this a mode of being that more completely—is this
a corrosive substance or isn't it is this a careful gesture is this a hard gesture
is this a complicated gesture, shove it—

by which one might deviate. is there a different way of doing this this is
haphazard this is pathetic in the interim where we wait this is dire also
luxurious this is an endless buzzing in ears this is a sequence of events

is this a disaster is this disastrous are you a monster yes you are monstrous
this is a vault where we keep the jewels this is a field is this myopic

this is a not an allegation of truth this is not the body you are to have
you are to have no bodies they are to have no bodies this is a growl
in the middle of words

this is an infraction & it is liable this is an eye-full this is morning
is this a surgence is it resistance

is this or isn't it a way of changing perception is this in order, is this the order
or is it ordinary in the half-light or is it revolting it is a mouthful it is revolting
it is molting it is releasing some shimmering body into the hands of the state.

u drink [river] no
in [u] the form
[toxic] inmirrored
as seeking [touch]
no is a [lasso]
in relation [my]
damp & [swan]
u [eat] there 2.

this is toxic in
its [carbon] [crystal]
form pharmaceutical
in its chrysanthemum
smells like [money]
& like [fish] I
[drink] no in
[daylight] no
in [neon] I.

I give [this]
back – [poison]
in its sepals [bright]
[chewed] & am
farmed [there]
I can swim in
no [river] eat
no [seed] [drink]

u I am [still]
meaty tho.

& my cathedrals
bright w. [hormones]
crude [sky] [land]
be [my] [rich] [flesh]
my [stolen] my
chemosynthetic
[prism] re[coil]
I swim in this
[river] u [drink]
from form I
give – is [toxic]
my [touch].

.OXYSM GENETIC DRIFT & MUTE AS A FAT SEED, GNARLY ZOIA
U UNSEXED ANTECENDENTS FEVERISH W. CAPTIVITY, WORLD

-FLUID VERSE (PER) SAY O BIOME "SO ROMANTIC" SHOT.
& RUBBED AGAINST. HAVE U PEOPLED THIS DOMAIN
W. ANAMORPHS ERECT W. POLLEN.

O "MY LOVE" YR STRAPPING BIOLOGISM; CREATURED
IN TECHNOLOGIC WILD - U FLUMMOX'D DISCONCEALMENT

ALL "CHARTREUSE" & "NEUROLOGICAL." —NO EVOLUTION
IS COMPLETE, IRRADIATED PURE. U ZYGOTE U GILDED SYMPTOMATIC
URGE, TO WORLDING [HERE?]

THIS THE FOREST

khjou[o9u4L
;OJdalsfhoij
poi[N/OPIP
OI?>>>PO{
UHHOIUDS
MWO''IJOI
O''Ilostdaf;
mqoi7*&^H
;kjasdup7^I
UG;kk;ja;jha
J{(*)*&TOij
bkamdoiukj
nlkjsp'9(Iam
aMONKEY
@#BKJC:W
TOleopard
@%ak;jn}{n
;aSULCICC
HICWEBVS
9adinthefore
stsfnl;ku;aoy
we&*%&6rf
jasel;87LIaa
&wer;IAMl
ostINTHEF
ORESTtryP
ANOPOelpt
IC@#UIDO
EOkjn;awiu
yvbYTR&%
E#na;jhPIU
TjasdcnIUZ

TouytY%#R
!akjbbYI&%
TShjkuytiat
OU^%hj;ku
U$*^EDLO
STIGOcraS
HIngthere@
$sgjhIT(*&t
TRUELYU
%&*%$EU
$%%IUY*
%^%#%&$
#^^T*&%*I
NTHEJGofo
reST!utoihb
aiutUVJHBk
;uyouar76e^
DUKHB:KjI
amaMonKE
YIN8dyfore
ESTvjlhbHL
KHWEhuiy
oufgdk;sj6T
$W^UTP(*
&^^&$@u6
hlkajsgdv5e
ygsvefa;kqu
mN*)&^zIA
MAMONK
EY%jkhSD
KJN;KJHkjh
knadvuytiwy

rerbkj12tefh
IAMAMonk
EYINTHEF
ORESTo;iw
herISwhereI
SITT#n;liY
OURY(*^@
Jk;hjvoisusaj
khmOIYKJ
Blkjo[aiehfk
jnqsl;fkupiu
5$^%ERIuh
IAMAMON
KEYINTHE
FORESTW
HEREARE
YOU>/?LO
Q*WYE/?J
Hwr37tawfj
bLYRYEwq
3utiyE$#@^
%(p87qwdkj
hiy!$#biopol
iticalTHIsIA
MlosTinTH
EForEST;ku
y;asdkjhUO
Ttet4wj4w3
75^#IAmaM
onKEYINT
HEFOREST
RYWHERE

AReyOU?E
?LUW?WU
ETUE^%#a
kjshfdkbu$T
^%#ISHOU
LDnwerv;iu
yerGHaveUI
TYcomEDO
NwonFROY
UIMTHEOI
YFTREWE
ESOUTQW
Eblkhr3ou64
^%#^$%#Y
$Wasgjfgjhi
duryUdfadh;
flkajS;LCK
XLMCN;K
UYLAKJFY
IYRTUHG'
LOEOPRQ
U7ER4#@$
^Z#!Iamana
monkheouti
bnkjtjyuinth
e;hFOihwer
kjhstIAMam
onekhgioyti
ntheFOREa
wsestiaMA
NOMonEKy
einIOYOnth

eFOIREST
W{YHEreA
IUrOYTOY
?{PI{P(o8w
ehkljgqewr;j}
{Pouypqw
73t;IAMfulk
jwe;jhfoffdie
siureIamfull
ofdesirewIa
ml;ifuiouylll
oOIfDeqsiri
hieruhekIO
UTAloiyMK
AYI76KLJH
UAO^$^%#
86734ijk;jt7
6$^lhj;YUO
KJKAJHER
PIULKLkhj
kj;lakshfiuyI
ljhiutIOAM
}{Ptu8o7w3
rhQ@?#$U
UIAMfuLLI
OFDESIREI
AMFULLao
ihjfijlijljkeoi
OHIUIamA
MOnkeyINt
hefoREStIA
MFullOFDE

SIREWHER
EaareyoU.?j
ahoesi?><W
QERout_)(^
@?Iamlafioi
mfmanaiO:J
mano;iuTU^
$^%@lUAI
AMAmANo
uiseonm,ouy
oiImalkmP(
&&*$^wkej
rkutC^#$Ia
ma(*^^E$M
ANINTHEF
ORESsTetoi
utqe4rlnIOO
HOheqnu%#
UYgkjhewkj
kjLKHAS:K
FJHUTUW
Yiut53^&$#
%^TNKLJG
&*(*AIMa
maMONKE
Yinthefores
TDESIRETi
ntheforeSTT
T!![9%&^$
@%wqejhcj
xzhgkyWZ$
^@67q34Be

IamLKJAmI
UmaMAonk
eyInTHeFOr
esSSTYIam
aMObkewni
uytiYTiNthe
foreEStIAM
amonkYEyi
nINTHEfore
stiIAMasnM
OanIAMEM
ANINTHthe
FOrewestTR
OreFOrestI
AMEIaMam
aNINthefoiF
OREsttIOTJ
IT&#KIIAM
AManINThe
FOFrest!IA
MaonkeyiNt
hefoRewstO
UTIAWUnl
kjdlfkgiAMa
MONkeytoiI
NTHEFORE
STIAMlosat
inlostlooostl
OstintheFOr
estIamOUT
MONkeytoiI
NTHEFORE

STIAMlosat
U$354y$*^
%#^n;lk"N
KHBnlmsdfl
knxknkjhiuT
RUTHFULL
YIasdmYES
weoiNK:AS
Fjfn;ual;ksd
AMFULLof
DesIREIAM
IAMFulloF
DESIreInthe
FORESTWh
ereSAREyo
OU?}{jkw;r
8&aetjIama
MANIaseral
kjIOAMIA
MamMANN
ainthEeFore
stIamlkostlo
stIAmlostIA
MAmanIA
MAMONK
EYInthefoF
REStXTRU
ThfullyIAM
aMANIamlo
stInthEFOre
sstin;:}xylo:i

[P Y X]

:::'"':L"sayfo
wlFOWLwo
lfOWL"{{{:
:vieVINEYe
'dDoe;;(::Th
istheFORES
Tfull"'"':R;W
E{{WASPp
edOWraBBI
THAREgrO
USE||grA{S
S;l;i]oOthef
ORESTickT
Hick::WOL
Fh/unt{edF
OX{}[[:OX/
enOZ?SWA
MPmos()&q
uito}::O;;M
APLESAP:;
;(WE)tbaRK
doEy:edST
AR:;;]BLAc
kTrUMPEt
CHanterEL
LES&swalL
OW.asPs"::
EYedWolfe'
dDOeBluES
KyintTHe:;i
nthFoRESt'
sTEETH!

Queerne
ssnecessi
tatesarad
ilcalizedl
anguage
basedint
hedissol
utionofth
eboundar
iesthatus
uallycirc
learound
concepts
thereisan
ecessary
displace
mentand
ambigou
szoneflu
xuatinga
roundthe
relations
hipsbetw
eensubje
ctsandob
jectssign
sandsign
ifierscon
ceptsofb

eautysex
ualitybo
diesbodi
nessemb
odiednes
simplicit
(madeex
plicitand
ambigou
s)gesture
sgenders
etc.none
ofwhichc
anbeund
erstooda
nylonger
asnatural
orunders
tandable
exceptinr
elationto
thefluida
ndtrembl
ingboun
darieszo
nedaroun
dtheman
ycentere
dselvedn
essesofsu
bjectivit

y/Ifqueer
nessinsti
gatesther
adicalres
hiftingan
dunderm
iningofre
cievedva
luationan
dhierarc
hythenits
underlyi
nginstabi
lityshoul
dupsetth
efoundat
ionsofthe
actofvalu
ingaltoge
therthusc
onstraint
saroundd
esiringbe
comeeph
emeralan
doneissu
bjectotot
he"bloo
mingbuz
zingconf
usion"of

anuncon
ceptualiz
edbeinga
washinth
esensesa
ndforced
tolookdif
ferentlya
tthevario
usdesires
sensation
sariseinu
s/thusge
net'sfilth
becomes
beautybe
autybeco
mesconf
oundeda
ndfreakis
hlyfreea
ndunbrid
ledtofor
mthechai
nsrosesth
espitrose
spearlset
c/onceth
ereisnoin
herenttru
throotedi

espitrose	itiontoit/	dissolve	dimplicit	onewithi	aneously
spearlset	azonewh	d?Merle	indefiniti	nwhichth	creating/
c/onceth	erelangu	auPonty	venessan	evibratin	Everyon
ereisnoin	agebreak	writesof	dthereexi	gmultipli	eknowst
herenttru	sdownint	Cezanne	stbynece	citiesofb	hatlangu
throotedi	operciev	(re:outlin	ssitylang	eingsmig	ageis"br
narigidid	ednongra	es)"Fort	uageacts	htattemp	oken"{w
eaofnatu	mmatical	heworldi	whichact	ttospeak	hichit'sn
reazonei	nonsensi	samassw	withinco	ortodefin	ot}butqu
serected	calnonsi	ithoutga	mmuniti	etheirow	eeredlan
outsideof	gnificati	psasyste	esforwho	nspeakin	guagean
'tovillify	onwhichi	mofcolor	mnormal	g/theima	danylang
'or'tosan	satthehea	sacrossw	izedspee	ginaryw	uagethat
ctify'the	rtofevery	hichthere	chimplic	orldnece	peoplcon
beingofa	humanan	cedingpe	itsacomp	ssitatedb	structfort
nykindof	waybutw	rspective	licityton	ybeingco	hesmelv
beingcau	hatlangu	theoutlin	ormalize	nfinedto	esoutside
ghtaswea	agenorm	esangles	dvalues/t	adefined	ofandaga
reinthem	alizesint	andcurve	heforceo	bodyandi	instforce
eshesofa	olassosar	sareinscr	forderbr	nadefine	dorenor
mediated	oundbod	ibedlikel	okennotb	dworldp	milizeds
worldbut	ies/How	inesoffor	ychaosb	utsonein	peachdo
ourexiste	canweev	cethespat	utbyarad	abizzarer	esn'tdisi
nceremai	entalkab	ialstructu	icalsubje	elationto	ntigratei
nssomeh	outsimpl	revibrate	ctiveamb	un/orhyp	ntononse
owoutsid	ethingsw	sasitisfor	iguitywh	er/orsur/r	nsebutin
eitImight	hensmall	med."/T	erelangu	ealit(ies)	steadinto
sayeveni	andsimpl	hereisfor	agebreak	inwhich	newantih
nqueerne	ewordsli	ceimplici	sitselftoc	weareen	ierarchic
ssdirectl	keprono	tinthislan	reateanin	mesheda	alwaysof
yinoppos	unshave	dscapean	terstitialz	ndsimult	sensing

	SISFULLOFC	ESTISFULLO
	ELLSTHISFO	FSTONETHIS
	RESTISFULL	FORESTISFU
	OFTHEACTO	LLOFURANIU
	FEATINGTHI	MTHISFORES
	SFORESTISF	TISFULLOFW
	ULLOFHYPH	ARMBLOODE
THISFORESTI	AEANDMYCE	DCREATURE
SFULLOFQU	LLIUMTHISF	STHISFORES
ARKSANDGL	ORESTISFUL	TISFULLOFE
UONSMUONS	LOFINSECTS	YESTHISFOR
ANDSUBATO	THISFORESTI	ESTISFULLO
MICDUSTTHI	SFULLOFWIN	FSOCIETIEST
SFORESTISF	GSFULLOFLE	HISFORESTIS
ULLOFCARB	AVESSOILDI	FULLOFFISH
ONBONDSM	RTNUTSSEED	ANDFISHER
AGNETISMPR	STHISFORES	MENTHISFOR
OTONSANDN	TISFULLOFH	ESTISFULLO
EUTRONSTHI	YDROGENOX	FSONNETSTH
SFORESTISF	YGENNITRO	ISFORESTISF
ULLOFAMOE	GENCARBON	ULLOFUULA
BAANDPARA	DIOXIDEMET	TIONSTHISF
MECIUMTHIS	HANETHISFO	ORESTISFUL
FORESTISFU	RESTISFULL	LOFCITIESCA
LLOFPROKAR	OFEXCRETIO	RSPLANESEN
YOTICFUNGI	NSANDINHA	GINESOILFIE
BACTERIUM	LATIONSTHI	LDSCROPSC
ANDSYMBIO	SFORESTISF	OMMERCEHI
SISTHISFORE	ULLOFBRON	STORIESTHIS
STISFULLOF	ZETHISFORE	FORESTISFU
MOLECULE	STISFULLOFI	LLOFSEXTHI
SMEMBRANE	RONTHISFOR	SFORESTISF

ULLOFROAD	ORESTISFUL	ESTSHURRIC	ZEDCRIMET	ITTHISFORES
STHISFORES	LOFMONEYA	ANESTSUNA	HISFORESTIS	TISFULLOFLI
TISFULLOFF	NDMETABOL	MISTORNAD	FULLOFSTOC	GNINLICHEN
LOWERSFUL	ISMSTHISFO	OESFLASHFL	KMARKETSA	ANDMOSSTH
LOFURGESF	RESTISFULL	OODSBLIZZA	NDNUMBERS	ISFORESTISF
ULLOFECON	OFOPPRESSI	RDSTHISFOR	THISFORESTI	ULLOFBITTE
OMIESSTATE	VEVALUESY	ESTISFULLO	SFULLOFHU	RNESSTHISF
SANDREGIM	STEMSTHISF	FBIRDSISFUL	NTERSANDP	ORESTISFUL
ESTHISFORE	ORESTISFUL	LOFBRANCH	REYTHISFOR	LOFPSYCHO
STISFULLOF	LOFDESIREIS	ESISFULLOF	ESTISFULLO	ANALYSISISF
BUILDINGST	FULLOFSCIE	RADIOWAVE	FTANKSTHIS	ULLOFPSYC
OOLSANDINF	NCEISFULLO	SANDELECT	FORESTISFU	HOSISTHISFO
RASTRUCTU	FTELESCOPE	RICCURRENT	LLOFSUSTIN	RESTISFULL
RETHISFORE	STHISFORES	SISFULLOFT	ANCEFULLO	OFNERVOUS
STISFULLOF	TISFULLOFE	EETHANDEA	FSPACETHIS	SYSTEMSFUL
MATHTHISF	YESTHISFOR	RSANDNOST	FORESTISFU	LOFMUCOUS
ORESTISFUL	ESTISFULLO	RILSISFULLO	LLOFDESIRE	FULLOFDISE
LOFGEOMET	FTASTEBUDS	FPEOPLETEL	FULLOFMET	ASETHISFOR
RYTHISFORE	ANDDEADSK	EVISIONSAN	AMORPHOSI	ESTISFULLO
STISFULLOF	INCELLSTHIS	DIRRIGATIO	SFULLOFLAR	FSTINGINGBI
ADRENALIN	FORESTISFU	NISFULLOFG	VAEFULLOF	TINGCLAWIN
EOXYTOCIN	LLOFCAPITA	ESTUREANDI	NESTSANDD	GGNASHING
NOREPINEPH	LTHISFORES	NTONATION	ENSANDMAT	RIPPINGROA
RINESALIVA	TISFULLOFLI	THISFORESTI	INGRITUALS	RINGCHEWI
ESTROGEND	BRARIESAND	SFULLOFLAN	THISFORESTI	NGSTALKIN
OPAMINETES	POLICEISFUL	GUAGEANDS	SFULLOFAD	GFEARFULC
TOSTERONES	LOFIMAGESF	YNTAXISFUL	ORNMENTISF	REATUREST
ALINESOLUT	ULLOFSOUN	LOFOBJECTS	ULLOFEXCH	HISFORESTIS
IONENZYME	DSFULLOFAI	ANDRATIOSI	ANGESISFUL	FULLOFSUFF
STHISFORES	RRAINCLOU	SFULLOFOR	LOFSEEKING	ERINGTHISF
TISFULLOFG	DSWINDCUR	GANIZEDAN	THISFORESTI	ORESTWASN
ENDERTHISF	RENTSTEMP	DUNORGANI	SFULLOFFRU	EVEREMPTY

```
                              ..';1} {PO}Pl
                              ""POLYP/';.
                              ;,]pk[pl} {P}
                              {}:"">":<'l[l
                              ,'l[][{PO{_s
<><<<<?>"                     ea::<o][p]=}
"":>>??":""                   P{L":K"po[;
"":/.;';'[][                  '.,';1[]_O+{
]{}{][;';'.}{;                )I[pl';.}{OI
'.,,][p;>>>>                  U)*(][p][][P
P}{'.';][_);'                 ';';l';';'AL
}|';1|\\":Lo)(               GAEICl;;":L
*}{+==?>?>                     [p';l"::,';,'p
<?></.+_}{p                  o{PU:RGE}
;'><>?;>?/.,.                {P][\|}[\>>][
'"::';<>":[]}                 {PO{'l;..';':
{}[.]["??>.'_                L"SA::RXa"
)9;)(_*()l;'"                :l][pSIL;;"P
}{}{}*0*][:                  {"';l':"][][';;
L;)O;1/.":}{}                .,<,,/><?>]/;l
][;.;l.[';';"]>               'l.,?><":l['pl
<>,/..,/..,/..><             }{[]][.]MYR
><M><M><                     IIACEA}{P
?.,[][>>.>>,]                ][}{)NAKE
[[][\>>\][]":                D":oP""|]/<"
[][\";1';1]\\][              :'[POLIS.>>
\][[p][p][p]"                :{P}{}][[op
:L[\][\[p]\[p]               olis}{!}[][]]
[][;][o][o\]>                [}{][}{}{;'O
?</,.,'p[][p":               PO'[p[]POp
LP{O{p;l';,/                 p[PO[pOPu
```

LENT/.NA
KED][][pPO
LIS!><>]][.]
[]?>ooohHH
HHH]][]{}{.,
[]><::PESTI
LENTOPUL
|ENTPOLIS
!][o{][op}[e[
N[EMB/::ar]
[ASSEDEU
KARYOKTI
CPOLIS!}{]
]OOpOPE{P
p[[]en]N]]O
p}e[]::|armi
l\laria/{}.S[c
//{}cll"ERE
CT;;[p]][&O
RedORDER
EDRATION
ALITY][]p[.
,[]\ERECTS
ASTATE}{.
l[][pl'!HUZ
ZAH;']][><.
,][!CHELIS]
[:TIC/LEUC
]][[?>SETW
.PEARLS&
BERRIES]][]

,;l][];.,m[p][]
o1oWILDL
YGENITAL
EDPOLIS:;,
[p}{P][p][][]
:][.][.,.;;;'{';]
CLANDEST
INEINTHE
CITY][><][)
(][};o1EXIS
TENTIAL][
OO';l][][PL
{P][][,ooUN
GARLAND
EDPOLIS][l
;lo1o[]oo1N
AKEDLYE
LECTRICO
NTHEINTE
RNET010[{
[][0]BinOMi
alEMBRAC
EGLOBLU
LAR&ANA
RCHICPOL
ISENCIRCL
INGTHEGL
OBE]][p[;.'p
]][p][,010Op
en{}.FLESH
EATER[o][;

l'.';l]THINS
KINNEDFI
SCALCRISI
SSOFTFLE
SHEDPOLI
S}{;.][DEN
DRITIC[];.'
WARMBLO
ODED[p[[0
10pBLOOD
IED"010{po
01OPOLIS)]
0PARASITI
CMATHEM
ATICS!01]0
01][0BAMB
OOZLEDO
OZINGPOL
IS)!])1][01][
0]1]PSYCH
OLOGICDR
EAMOFPU
PAE}0}{0O
oBIOPOLIT
ICALPOLIS
W.PSYCHO
LOGICALM
AMMALIA
NDREAMS
OFTHEOPU
LENTCITY

. }} :+
+-_ - ...
:} {*((o ^^
!" .
.| | | |/*(%$
&>>
>>o:
:::::: fulc }}:
_= daedalic
i{< >>> *
arch•ambryo
nic*>>>ick)
)) <.,. o|o
uulogi..>.*ir
-izon ++++
#>>..} }\
v.}_
>>plz<<ver|
}iliy///|}}+_:
diamond_tru
eilicPlz)>>I
amnotaLiar)
))h|ow?>.}|}
}_))><<>;'
+ +)_|}{
+++
- >. . /';
'}][$ +
>>
_l>>

>>:._---.
/?}..
../;ARK\o;>
oz::'
>:__-_
%volt%-+
*.)90(*)))^lo
ve..void>>io
d>))}"is"..}]
]>>Xin>Tru
th% plz>}
-&*0
>..)}[
{
..
//,,}
]D(.
.>..l;
o;l,/,;'. euph
Oric}[[melli
floric}]>...{-
,.m0-..[]ozic
/>.,,./[{little.
./..,bell&•rin
ging><.[-
>>,;[}0
][;:;
;'
::;.>glycy]}[
00:.>lion>'))
)^hea•vy]w.f
ur///soft}}w.

fur..:}[.
.,{">< '}\
][] 0-=-
=_+
+
_
+ +-
)(
(•)))))
.
. . .
. .
. 0.,. 0
)- =%
+ +
>>idyl..)(litt
le][><.wildg
oat>ortendril
} {0verily..."
:..'[|}-*
}}=
*^>,
,..,?plz.>.:ve:
see:"{.><:::;
:ooo
}}{};+/.,my
?><love:<>)
(&*><..,.<<
<is><;o*(&^
%><>/.//soft
>/w.fur..,/.))
(little}} {]rin

ging} {.>/ver
ily../../..><>
a|bell>.,"';in
me.?/?>?.?>.
,.this:_+
_)+- =
-+_ is
+_lu
dicrous&.<>
solemn..<,.in
{}>
?<+=-/.
>,/:
[][]=*0(<>}
the?world?>
> > < "..)|>
*%>>";';";"
":';>...._0>>
>..<><

IT DOESN'T CURE IN ITS SOCKET

I.

trespass

     this is an illegitimate Eurydice

    <>

-onymny   polyurethaned eyelids in sleep
the bulls are claustrophobic, ringing.

one might be nasty, but one might be one]naked
]archambrionic]inmooned-aggregating]yellow-breasting

I am in the petaluminescent excrementious void of a reply—

    <>

swim with me in the river

    <>

       out into]sheaves]from out of]like rain]harm come

obliquely shielded carapace
    throbbed in the rock outside of me

<>

signet hollow of a tree limb'd occularist hype   slick w.
        ]hand benumbed –   joist

knotted red to tongued eyelet   actual rib

<>

"throbbed in the rock outside of me"
        I could feel it there   ]outside of me   ] throbbing

<>

the hoofed red-meat stands steaming in the field

<>

docilely

    a honeyed cut   ]abscess in-branch]in pinkish-tinged rafter

the punctured in-dom's averted gaze   elixed me
to a nest there   sugar suspended in fat]captivation]is the sun of a made
thing

nest me down in the cycloptic aperture;

    & "whoever looks in the open sees only a closing, only a not-seeing"

II.

       golden-headed joy of the warbling cock[dom] // [the rough
rose & pileated sun]   sparred   bright by void, foil, coin.

      <>

       dense/amass in ultraviolet lit. contingent human   this inde-
cent . "to summer in" &beta, coil, swarm.

      <>

       sing: "ular" - vis. insouciant vitality//come softly. "what
about masculine v. feminine postures" ballerina: come among the insouciant
flowers limp & bare.

      <>

       be ridden in necessity, sewn & crowned gems. [jubilation]
[to pitch skyward] hornless, bright. diadem the soft cleaved warm & wrung

      <>

   & has no world but this.

III.

<>

                                        loudly came a clanging
hoarse in velvet   in cunning : all is, or isn't.   all irises are   or isn't— real
season a happening in form   absconsive, diurnal, gestate, symph.   by brittle

                                    :stem is hour's sweet a fleeting
     while they flower sweat the only gesture : versus human   :   per/
verse, us, human   the only pasture is dug up: open   like a chord.

                              all the revolting   : reared up &
into,   "over" "through" "within" ,   & pears rot & so do lemons & dead
things left out in the sun, hum "harm" swarm what vital : vaulted   all veneer
a pearled ash to crust up on, time.   :each is a day : what does   it   ripen.
or doesn't—

                        all aspartame in bleach   : "effluvium"   effeminate
pour sour over ocean   pour some "sugar on me" : full of graph all that slip all
sliding chemistry   : sound, body, versus "human" :   is & then later again   is
& then there is another   perennial   stipend to plow.

versus a loud abrasive   isle   sung "hung"
hanged what cured : reviled at a touch summer   nighting over   all slip
all   slipped the distance :   veered   "versus" human : "sun", "tree",
"asphalt", "fault", "name", "pattern", "ocean".   endurance :   measured in
limits   litmus : electric   honey   baby   mine.

<>

GUNOILEDSUNOILEDGUNOILEDSUN.

1. trespass to Land.

frond w. tiara. Tiara in the pasture The wide cheek of pasture. flock. deer.
safety/ hazard. spoiled. the edge of the boundary of is slick w.
permission.

2. swoon

swoon in the criss cross & swoon the irrelevance . & swoon &
brace under. & swoon & rear up. the trees are the eyelashes of creeks.

3. Treason

is vagrancies Circlet. leap/leapt "across" mud encircled by shine. I am
amphitheater in Throne / enthroned & Thrown there—unspecific as ferning
ferns fear The wind borne spores a Flock & settles. makes of the air an
intermingling/ is this a violence

is canopy. the open eyes of ponds. will answer.

4. is given Over

lest u mistake my antiphony. erect is as justice is across
the wide expanse of pasture Wherein several flocks unveil to hazard
is a sewn, unknown thing is as in the seeping

as in the weeping
fuck yr willows
deer meat my quivering
derservation How has this entered here

5. designates a space Surrounded

hawk me an eyeball beak is a gun there. slick in the aquifer & slick
to cut the sugar thru the hollow the relentless through the chosen the
endless to cut the arteries from my endless my arterial trees. dense &
tangle there is as slipping between with their delicate & their lashes.

  slipping as if they don't know the difference between Here and There— as if
they have never heard
of "wilderness"— (of "Sovereign"—)

6. my Angel

my bright gun is oiled is pulses through an aquifer what is your name. is this
my is dear
is mine is my tiara encircling there.

is enclosed me is when is pierced You fawns timid w. knowing.

vis. obscene cult   // it is errored there
"rivelabilità" <<psuedobiologia>>

grass me Hyacinthine / Apollo'd
desire—

•

"all growed up": & tangled: all flagrant
"en flagrante"

each tawn & iance deep
& purple snag

wreak havoc plum aphro-delphinium in.
.iolet in need. // fetished gorgéd spring—

indecent in genetic shock all
cherish'd muscled sprung

•

(o)Zephyr— (lace)erate u vile blue-as-a-deep
in "wild" is brute x(tasy) gleaning
the ripe aspect of a pink-tipped sky—
is (sa)tin my star(ling) in (c)lover

{by necssity • embedded • embodied • necess
ity • embedded • clover • erase over • laid <laid on
top of> • [laden] • erasure • vibrating • lover • dissolv
ed • land/scape/me • subjectless wind • mis/place/
d • de•sire(d) "all over" • AS XRONOS THRU HIR B
ALLSAC 2 THE HEAVENS; SPEWED THE MILKYWA
Y ACROSS THE NIGHT & HUNG NECLACED THERE
• overfull • displaced <unbounded> desire • resoundin
g • ZOUNDS! • Hopkins: "KISSED THY ROD/I WRETCH LAY WRES-
TLING WITH" • U FAGGY SISSY • NECKING THE [GOD/
HEAD] • go • go into • go deep into • go into the deepening •
go unlace the deepening field • &gently • go
erase yr body into the deepened field•}

•

"brill"   trophic bios
sacre "sac" shugar from
hymenium & "milky way" u erratic
& whimsical aphrodisiac

bios (o) u well hung [horses] u
frivolous filthy menace 2 form / "sugar sugar"
hype all plume

& clawed arrival. "U PEACH U MINX U
SKANK U PETAL, BITCH" adorned. the soft
& daggered   //   bulls of dawn.

{т(REASON)}

.

the treasuries are faulty   like the earth   hermaphroditic
full of loiter & persuasion .

succession happens in the empty fields where small weeds
& nitrogen   "you climax to a forest"   full of bile & tiny blue

hand on limb   limb a flock   succulent dendrite   connects
where desire converges   antennae   plural & decibel   how we learnt it   by
force

like as if a river   "a" as in singular   "as if—"
is a ripped open stone   is overgrown   is iffy in the rigorous architecture

mock flensing   be bright uproot   be beaten into
what peach a flock will matter   a many tiered pulse

is seeded to be petulant an endemic   arboreal   caress
this is filthy soil   but beautiful—

rubix (f)lux = BIZZARE re-combination
stitch glo to a cell wall   glo [osis] is

   [god]less rapa[city] =
"the obliterating brutality of the natural world"
              alive = alive

snarky "logic". this is a "locatable region" cut, swathed, tunneled,
drained, painted, raised, pitched, plumbed, hacked, scraped, channeled,
"glowed"—

    constructed wilderness   [.   ]

\

abandon   "reckless" verily
need { BLUER THAN } & bleed it—

hum [hope]less bird-brained mammalian brain
slithering between rot & abstraction :

    glo this my genetic triumph over night.

eden a den or eden city   hung there this hex
-agonal my bionic blue
                              -vivanate encrusting
        lupine   hush   down
        yes it is

    bleat to, beaten—gimme—sunshine—hollowing— fovic—latencies
        so excessive—my—

"rammed earth"

            stimulus electricity molecule striation
            morbidity nonsense gelatin actuality

        monstrous capital rhizomic rut

clusterous aggre/gate form from complete what var. like it
                be thorough in yr—

    [bile, not against, nature]

be it rooting there   too euph/oric culprit bleat   for it, choose
                be a zoic version, sucker, salt fiend—

unrhyme as optic, is as, be.

{EVERYTHING THAT IS BEAUTIFUL IS EDIBLE}

      ungodly ugly marsh marigold
maximillian & appled   "diuretic love, criminal
castled harvest"   transgressive & unpeopled domain

"pummeled" *to fall thru the ripened skin* a landscape
is a volatile animal   median, axon, circumference
     gravity causes the heavy fruits to fall

but to see the arc of spin we have to hurl them hard—

        pelvic, or dactylic, "gnawed"
noxious & bitter populace . *spoilt cerebellum feasted* "given"
   sanguine ox-eye I'll roll over promise

   "obey"—   I am in the eye of the blossom.

{THEFT}

sun me a helmet—gross bloodlet—clover all
is purloined touch of heat & pink in spurn

leave it to rot. I grab
my balls & throw
a starling.

bitter obstruction along the carapace.
climbing hysteria so beautiful so yellow

all is velvet in the cuts & all culled sky is abscess
& all is sullen—this gear—slag of muscled bone.

I is a single discomposure in the intermittent landscape.

unravel me a harness—sudden pitch—snag
in the orifice—vine is leeway—jewels of it

I is a single decomposure
happen to skin me an eye.
happen to steal it back.

[MYTILOS] // [MYX]

u cultivate the xerox of a zero is a foraged glycogen I've hunted there.

a sought thing in the seeking as sweet is in the tasting—

} this is a telescope in which I am omitting something important.

u grow perverse w. being in the perversity of being. I imagine myself into
the hunt in the reality of the hunted molecules which are now binding into long
strands there.

{the phantoming of limbs// the imagined limbs inside the limbs // the imag-
ined limbs extend beyond the body} : I am libidinous in my syntax & gluttonous
in my forms, however,

I reign in as a disciplined restraint—

        }   hunger in the cardiac
        }   hunger in the thoracic
        }   hunger in the deepening field

{ perplexed in hyperbolic   // foolish in paroxysm // lustful in proximity }

u convert the glucose into shimmering chains I wrap around my anthem.   de-
clension in the very mirror the imaginary stands erect & is a universe.

} this is the only habitable region in the whole valley –

{if the mind is embedded in the body & the body is embedded in the world}
{if the mind extends beyond the body & is defined as the intermingling of the
body & the world as sensed in the sensing of that intermingling} {if we can
have imaginary sensations that exist in our real imagined bodies} {then}   there
is an animal in my throat, etc.

　　} & each must be reimagined in relation to the world

u graft u sow u pull & from the depths there. I have been a made thing & a
hunted thing. the oaks bear pears in the deepest recesses. the sap runs salty
there.

　　} this is the sovereignty implicit in illegal & nonsensical acts

　　} this is an inescapable collision in the real

is the limbing of the imagined thing the being of the being of positing oneself
in the between between the world & the body—

　　} sweetness imagined as communication between
　　　animal & plant

　　} what is omitted is a profusion // is permission there—

{in the hyperoxygenated air // in the hyper-realities of nerve layer on nerve layer // in the irrelevance of boundaries // outside whatever crystalline amorphous helixed struggle there conceived as bondage is now dissipating in the breeze // sporulating // is a pulsing in & of the world its many coppiced self & twined there}

my love is a mimicry cultivated in deep shade in brightest hours.

u mockery of the natural forest in rock grown hot pink in crystal sugar I have excreted beyond my molecular structure the shafts of sunlight pressing into the forest there. I have halted & thudded in exchange for the prey I am after there. this is deep in the collusion of bodily forms—

GET OUT // MY FACE: U centaur in yr accident // corrosive in yr
gendered unicorn be all like fuck you in my pink quartz diodes I'll jizz in my
own ~~paradise~~ • in the semirigid vesicles u orchard there all mythic in yr verge
& verging method, flexed.• the pain is a deep verb deep in yr metabolism // is
a phenotypic gemstone u chickenhawk u falcon repugnant in my masculine
~~love~~ —

ALL MY HEROES ARE CRIMINALS— Is the dawn lucrative in yr cellulite
u corpulent garden // in anger // Victory • in pastoral • x-rated yr [my] showy
hackles there all "crepuscular" & "range" • I am as a ragged edge in this [yr]
[our] dimension is a fist of noise I place hard in the bulging geometry // I wanna
fight "man to man" in yr deep // throat my ~~song~~.

NO KING W/O A CROWN :   Yr lactating in yr cock-eyed biceps
transcribing // transversing form u boar-taint in my [your] fuchsia plumage I'll
eat you alive u beautiful u beefy of suffering • u ~~estrogenic~~ pluot "deceptive"
uppercut in the fleshy street // cusp in my inner dilation // • u rival the
enjambment • u catalysis in my recognizance, recognized, & standing, there—

HOLD ME // BACK— Is wracked w. sobs in the interstice // u fisted
morpheme terse in yr [my] restraint • caustic in yr musculature • a scar in yr
larynxed ~~minotaur~~ is like shut the fuck up // is a trembling in yr juxtapositional
// in yr [my] insurgence • is my coveted [my] ripped [form].

["*LET US INQUIRE, TO WHAT*
END IS NATURE?"]

liq::
::cur
ovb::
:lol:

::

TUBERS GROW UNDERGROUND. SOME
MUSHROOMS START AS EGGS.
PARASITIC BRAIN FUNGUS IS A REAL
THREAT FOR ANTS. SOME PEOPLE
SURVIVE OFF OTHER PEOPLE'S
GARDENS.

::

::alb
::luv
zzz::
mur::
xot::
ix::

::

PLUMS ARE COVERED IN NATURAL
YEAST. FUR IS MADE FROM REAL
ANIMALS. BODY ODOR COMES OUT

YOUR PORES. ALL GENDER IS
PERFORMANCE.

::

:crx
::sth:
:vie:
xxx:

::

IN TUCSON ALL THE ORANGE TREES
ARE ONLY ORNAMENTAL. TEARS
CONTAIN MANGANESE. IAMBIC
PENTAMETER IS AN ARTIFICIAL
STRUCTURE THAT RISES OUT OF
LATINATE INTONATION LIKE HOW
MATH RISES OUT OF THE INTER-
ACTIONS OF MATTER.

::

::lli:
::kzt:
:atg
ur&
lmt::

::

AN ORGANISMS PHENOTYPE IS NOT
DICTATED BY ITS GENOTYPE. HUMANS
PLAY MUSICAL INSTRUMENTS. NINETY
PERCENT OF CELLS IN THE HUMAN
BODY ARE NON-HUMAN MICROBES.

::

yr internal flora & fauna
is a veritable eden a lush
& thriving estuary.

::

vid::
li::m
gtt::
nies:
::fʋr
zli::
::pp

::

ECONOMIES ARE MADE OUT OF
PEOPLES DECISIONS. HUMANS ARE
ANIMALS. THE GREEN IN SNOT IS THE

SAME   BACTERIA   IN   ALGAE.
CHIMPANZEES   KILL   OTHER
CHIMPANZEES AND HAVE COMPLEX
SOCIAL   POWER   STRUCTURES
INVOLVING   SEXUAL   DOMINANCE

::

      delineation denotes belonging yr
      sweet loves, vivid disgusts.

::

vio
llv::
nt:li
ply
:cvd

::

      yes an amalgamation of bodies make
      what is "sexual constructivism"

::

::vvv
spk::
is:L

:iam:
:cnl:

::

EVERY ORGANISM HAS AN ENERGY
SOURCE.   THERE   ARE   CHEMO-
SYNTHETIC PLANTS AT THE BOTTOM OF
THE OCEAN FLOOR THAT NEVER GET
SUNLIGHT.

::

         in sun light warm &
is soft the

     mammalian brain all ps
ych o

    or onto logical seek.

::

::acg
t:::g
::tim
id::
ult::
ion::

::

INSIDE CHICKENS THERE ARE MANY
EGGS IN VARIOUS STAGES OF
FORMATION. HETEROSEXISM PER-
PETUATES THE MYTH OF MONOGAMY
AMONG SWANS. THIS IS ALSO THE
MYTH OF "PURITY." HOMOSAPIENS
PROBABLY INTERBRED WITH, AND
ALSO KILLED, NEANDERTHALS.

::

mute mutable trumpet genesis be
o ugly little duck stay ugly

::

::ill:
uck:
::yr:
::nlv
vrr::
:atu::

::

19 YEARS AFTER THE NUCLEAR
EXPLOSION AT CHERNOBYL "the sum effect
for the flora and fauna in the highly radioactive,

restricted zone has been overwhelmingly positive in favor of biodiversity and abundance of individuals." IN FOUR SUCCESSIVE GENERATIONS OF SELECTIVE BREEDING, WILD BOARS LOOK AND ACT LIKE DOMESTIC PIGS.

::

o monad genomic o O o O o O
oOoOoOoOoOoOoOoOoOoOo
OoOoOo hapless haploidial curr
corrosive mutagentle purr

::

::cct
cvt::
vll::
:ovl:
lvo::

::

ANIMALS EAT OTHER ANIMALS. MITOCHONDRIA IN HUMAN CELLS WAS ONCE A SEPARATE ORGANSM. SOME ANIMALS LIVE OFF THE ENERGY PRODUCED BY THE PHOTOSYNTHETIC ALGAE THAT LIVES INSIDE THEIR

TRANSLUCENT SKIN.

::   .

u sym u biotic u mut ant u mut ual
aid? no. u all cap ital & ex change.
I ♥ all para site. & all purr / loined
proto   zoic   zone   all   coin

::

:oor:
:lsy:
:yy:
zz::

::

THE   SECOND   LAW · OF   THERM-
ODYNAMICS STATES THAT IN ALL
ENERGY EXCHANGES, IF NO ENERGY
ENTERS OR LEAVES THE SYSTEM, THE
POTENTIAL ENERGY OF THE STATE
WILL ALWAYS BE LESS THAN THE
INITIAL ENERGY OF THE STATE. MA-
MALS SEEK WARMTH. SOME PEO-
PLE PAY OTHER PEOPLE TO CLEAN
UP THEIR OWN MESSES.

::

they say guns
        are the great equalizer.

::

:vilt
ooo:
:shh
ght:
:ong:

::

THE COLOSSEUM WAS BUILT BY
SLAVES. THE PYRAMIDS WERE BUILT
BY SLAVES. THE WHITE HOUSE WAS
BUILT "LARGELY" BY BLACK AFRICANS
FORCIBLY BROUGHT HERE AND
ENSLAVED. THE CORAL REEFS ARE
BUILT BY CORALS AND PROVIDE A
HABITAT FOR MANY SMALL FISH.

::

grinding [at] bit the [gleam] from
shale is hack [ed] fossil per [verse]
the blind, the blinding sum.

::

::agg
gct::
ccc::
::gc
:ttv:

::

BONES RECORD DIETS. ONE GENE ON
8% OF ALL Y CHROMOSOMES CAN BE
TRACED BACK TO MONGOLIA DURING
GENGHIS KHAN'S REIGN IN THE
ELEVENTH   CENTURY.   BONOBO
MONKEYS   ARE   DEEMED   INAPPRO-
PRIATE ZOO ANIMALS BECAUSE THEIR
SEXUAL PRACTICES REMIND US TOO
INTIMATELY   OF   OUR   OWN.

::

penultimate coreopsis velt be doe

be dismal doe does vile perm do sway

gall doe lilly strut & eat little leaf

::

::ggg
atg::
acc::
:ctg:
ggt::
:gut

::

DISGUST IS THE MECHANISM BY WHICH
SOCIETIES ENFORCE SOCIAL/MORAL
CODES. A RING SPECIES IS A GROUP OF
SIMILAR   ORGANISMS   THAT
INTERBREED   AMONG   THE
NEIGHBORING POPULATIONS BUT ON
THE OUTSKIRTS OF WHICH THERE
EXIST SOME POPULATIONS THAT ARE
TOO   GENETICALLY   DISPERSE   TO
INTERBREED   WITH   EACH   OTHER.

::

gasoline, palace
prius ipod cubic
zirconia halogen
ford F−9 million

::

::atp
tra::
clw:
:vux:
:ccc:

::

HUMANS EXPERIENCE PSYCHOLOGIAL
REALITIES AND LIVE IN
PSYCHOLOGICAL WORLDS. PINK WAS A
MANLY COLOR UP UNTIL THE TURN OF
THE 20th CENTURY. THE ALL FEMALE
WHIPTAIL LIZARD SPECIES
"Cnemidophorus neomexicanus"
REPRODUCES BY PARTHENOGENISIS.

::

vine m e a r i f e is livid i s v i s c o u s
be l i k e a s a p r e d a t o r y

minutia a l l f o r e n s i c and
g o w n e d as is g r o t e s q u e l y
necessary—

is as is vile is [the] only rifle be me as
vulgar is as—

mutant (thy) ~~hands~~.

[WHAT A WASTE IS MADE]

what waste is made of uncontrollable things. what manic needs a well fed violin. a sarcophagus for kings.

what imbecile untraded for oil in the heat's glimmer releases toxins, forms a mycorrhizal relationship to forms, trades furs for unprotected flesh & sings.

what ripe landscape resists a rig, what prince crust-jeweled is permitted [her] own buzzard economy, what irascible logic grows full &sweet. my hands are claws, no logic

trumps a psychological truth no trumpet relentless no weary shall no shelter.

:::

what limp or bare-backed bare-boned regalia is a throwback to a whip, crown, death-church. what individualist maniac gnaws on aesthetic purity in this hodgepodge hallelujia of spring. "is something like a phenomenon"

plato was a wuss in the face of the human mess. my godless eden grows semi-autonomous fruit. "take me back to the paradise city/ where the grass is green & the girls are pretty" how can you go out with such a messy face, girl. what burly spring finds me what edible permutation of a form.

is this it? is it a grief? is it a "wingéd thing"?

:::

what halter made for a blood-horse is rigged with wifi, pure gold antennae, what
is so vulgar about a flower, Pleurotis ostreotis & sod. (o, my)

is the flash flood a call to arms against an ocean? what about heterogeneity?
what triumph is hell-bent to revile a virile orchestra, what desire sires bulls,
bullies a fleshy pansy, what ochre breeds order. but seriously, would you kiss a
dude?

perverse analysis of sociological construct Venus my Argive what kingdom is
princely, what king-dom dung-dominion, what empire worth the price. would
you kill for it? how many for lack of it? "across the fruited plain" a place a
palace built for queens.

:::

radical ambiguity if taken seriously would dissolve "rationalist" structures
of division like "subject/object" "cause/effect" "mind/body/world" "he/she"
"right/wrong" "syntax/semantics" "supply/demand."

necessary & [sic] insufficient anatomy, what essentialist hides behind a
pseudo-linguistic fallacy, divinity, unfettered coffers, the larva bred of wealth
& cleanliness divines a moral code a codex a rolex an undefined, yet totally
"natural," sense of ease & clarity of motion through an otherwise dense &
impenetrable world.

let's cast aside these castrated lilies, slip out of this graceful masculinity, what
idyll is rough-hewn from raw cement, what cash is pure, what baboon erects a
monument to god— a monument of coin.

(Danae) "make it rain"

[BEAST REMIX]

BeAsT ShAkE ThIs CrUsT BeJeWlEd w. CoReOpSiS
& RoUgH ThIs DiRt EaRtH Up aLL RiPe w. SwEaT
ThIs LaNdFiLL ViSiOn ScAr-HoRiZoN DiS-
EaSe AlL Up In My MaNLy RhInEsToNe SwEeT

w. AlL ThE NoXiOuS HoNeY o SwEeT MeAt BeEs
Of BeAsTliNeSs AnD InDuStRy'S CoNcEiT
CoMe MuTaNt fLoRa'S UgLy PrOgEnY, KiSs
ThE sLiCk Of ThIs TrAnSgReSsIvE EaRth'S CoNcReTe.

YoU ArE aLL JuSt *AlMoSt* HuMaN. NoNeThELeSs,
Yr SaTiN, DaZzLeD FuR AnD ObScEnE SeCrEtIoNs
CaLL FoRtH ThE sMeLLs Of MoSs AnD PrAdA, PiSs
AnD LiChEn, LiStLeSs VuLgAr BeAsT aLL MeEk

BeFoRe ThE SuNsEt Or ThE GoD DaMn CaReSs
Of BeInG SePaRaTe, HeLd, MiMeD, GeMmEd, eLiTe.

AHSAHTA PRESS

SAWTOOTH POETRY PRIZE SERIES

2002: Aaron McCollough, *Welkin* (Brenda Hillman, judge)

2003: Graham Foust, *Leave the Room to Itself* (Joe Wenderoth, judge)

2004: Noah Eli Gordon, *The Area of Sound Called the Subtone* (Claudia Rankine, judge)

2005: Karla Kelsey, *Knowledge, Forms, The Aviary* (Carolyn Forché, judge)

2006: Paige Ackerson-Kiely, *In No One's Land* (D. A. Powell, judge)

2007: Rusty Morrison, *the true keeps calm biding its story* (Peter Gizzi, judge)

2008: Barbara Maloutas, *the whole Marie* (C. D. Wright, judge)

2009: Julie Carr, *100 Notes on Violence* (Rae Armantrout, judge)

2010: James Meetze, *Dayglo* (Terrance Hayes, judge)

2011: Karen Rigby, *Chinoiserie* (Paul Hoover, judge)

2012: T. Zachary Cotler, *Sonnets to the Humans* (Heather McHugh, judge)

2013: David Bartone, *Practice on Mountains* (Dan Beachy-Quick, judge)

AHSAHTA PRESS

NEW SERIES

This book is set in Apollo MT type
with Scala Sans titles
by Ahsahta Press at Boise State University.
Cover design by Quemadura.
Book design by Janet Holmes.

AHSAHTA PRESS
2014

JANET HOLMES, DIRECTOR
ADRIAN KIEN, ASSISTANT DIRECTOR

DENISE BICKFORD
KATIE FULLER
LAURA ROGHAAR
ELIZABETH SMITH
KERRI WEBSTER